Paint My Skin with Sweetness

Written by Cameron Chiovitti

Illustrated by Pamela Leszczynski

Table of Contents

What I'll Tell Her If She Reads This — 3
Rejection as the Hiccups — 5
Stopwatch — 6
A Series of Images — 10
One More Theory About Your Eyes — 13
Rejection as a Stray Cat — 15
Night Sky — 16
Ode to Camila Cabello Ending in a Swarm of Bees — 20
Drunken Ramblings of a Broken Heart — 23
Rejection as a Manic Episode — 25
Museum — 26
Instincts — 29
My Burgundy Dreams — 30
Rejection as a Drag Queen — 47
We Were All Just Stars on Fire — 48
If I Were an Artist — 53
13 Ways of Looking at a Memory — 54
Acknowledgements — 61
About the Author & Artist — 63

What I'll Tell Her If She Reads This

Don't worry, darling.
Just because I am writing about you now,
Does not mean I am still in love with you.
It's taken me many years,
But I no longer dream of kissing you.
You are merely the canvas onto which I will paint
The picture of my adolescence.
The picture of my adolescence is a bleak one,
But your curved edges make it a little softer.
See, loving you is what made me turn to poetry.
It is the only way I can even attempt
To uncover all the reasons I cared for you so.
I wish you all the best.
I mean, I wish you a museum of Monets.
I mean, I wish we could have found a way to stay friends.
I mean, I wish we were close enough friends that
I didn't have to write you this poem.

Rejection as the Hiccups

She breathes.

I breathe.

She breathes, harder.

I hold my breath,
But she keeps breathing.

I drink water,
But she keeps breathing.

I do whatever it takes
To get her to stop,
But all she is doing
Is breathing.

That's the thing with
Rejection;
We seem to make her so
Much bigger than she needs to be.

Stopwatch

Someone, somewhere, presses start on a stopwatch. Then, stop. Then, start. They find amusement in clicking and unclicking, unsure whether time does indeed start and stop with them.

START: She gives me a jellyband bracelet in the shape of a spider, not for the symbolism, but because her brother doesn't want it. I wear it every day for a year, even when it breaks.

STOP: The silence between us is so tangible, when I try to slice through it, the knife laughs.

START: We take the metro home together after school every day. She only lives two stops away.

STOP: Two desks over, she watches me watch her. Neither of us dares to blink. It is the only connection we have left.

START: She is a butterfly in a swarm of spiders. She is the one good thing about this place; the only thing gentle enough to love.

STOP: The spiders eat her alive. She becomes a shell of who she used to be, and cracks at the mere mention of how colourful her wings once were.

START: Every time I see her, I wonder how my heart can become a stopwatch and still pump so much blood to my face.

STOP: I doubt she has even given me a second thought since she saw me last.

START: She tells me she hopes, and she dreams, and I wish I can tell her I do too. About her.

STOP: She tells me I should speak to a therapist instead of her.

START: She loves me.

STOP: She loves me, but only as a friend.

START: It's the first day of gym class, and we are paired in the same group. She tells me her name and I smile. I know we are destined to be great together.

A Series of Images

My fingers graze
The daisies you planted in the park,
But they drip plasma onto their petals.

It burns when I pee
Because the blue jays
Are flying out of my urethra.

The snake tells me
It is foolish to write all these poems
About you.

I pluck the puffer fish
And I make myself
A necklace with its gills.

The ocean cannot hold
All of the waste this world has to offer;
It would merely poison her lungs.

The desk breaks, and all the books fly out.
One hits you in the head,
In hopes it will finally get you to look at me.

It's funny how
I still remember you
So fondly.

I chew on
The piano keys,
And they taste like mildew.

The leaf that crunches underneath my shoe
Had a mother, and that mother
Is underneath your shoe.

You find my sister's OPUS card in the grass,
But when she tries to pick it up, the bodies
Buried in the dirt grasp her by the wrist.

The air in between my bones
Cannot bear the pressure of your disapproving gaze;
They crack when your lips part.

At the end of the rainbow,
Instead of finding my pride, I find a note that says
Maybe you should go for a jog.

We dissect cow hearts in the same room,
And I wear the aorta as a ring
When what I really want to be wearing is the scalpel.

The red aura quartz cracks
In my pocket, and from it spills every drop of blood I've shed
in your name;
I am soaked from the waist down.

I rip the pages
Out of your favourite book
And fold them into an engagement ring.

Daily, I rip my jeans
By the seams
In hopes of making a blanket.

In a dream,
I walk up to you and kiss you,
Just because I can.

One More Theory About Your Eyes
After Paul Guest

That the pools
Of brown are a basin
Of dark chocolate,
That any child would dream
To swim in.

That the half-moons
From the flash
Of the phone camera
Will one day eclipse.

That, if each iris contains a snapshot of the soul,
Then your soul
Is a spring fox
Trotting along the golf course,
Just far enough away
To be marveled.

That each blink
Is shedding a leaf
From the tree of your past.

That, in the past,
They saw me,
And they smiled.

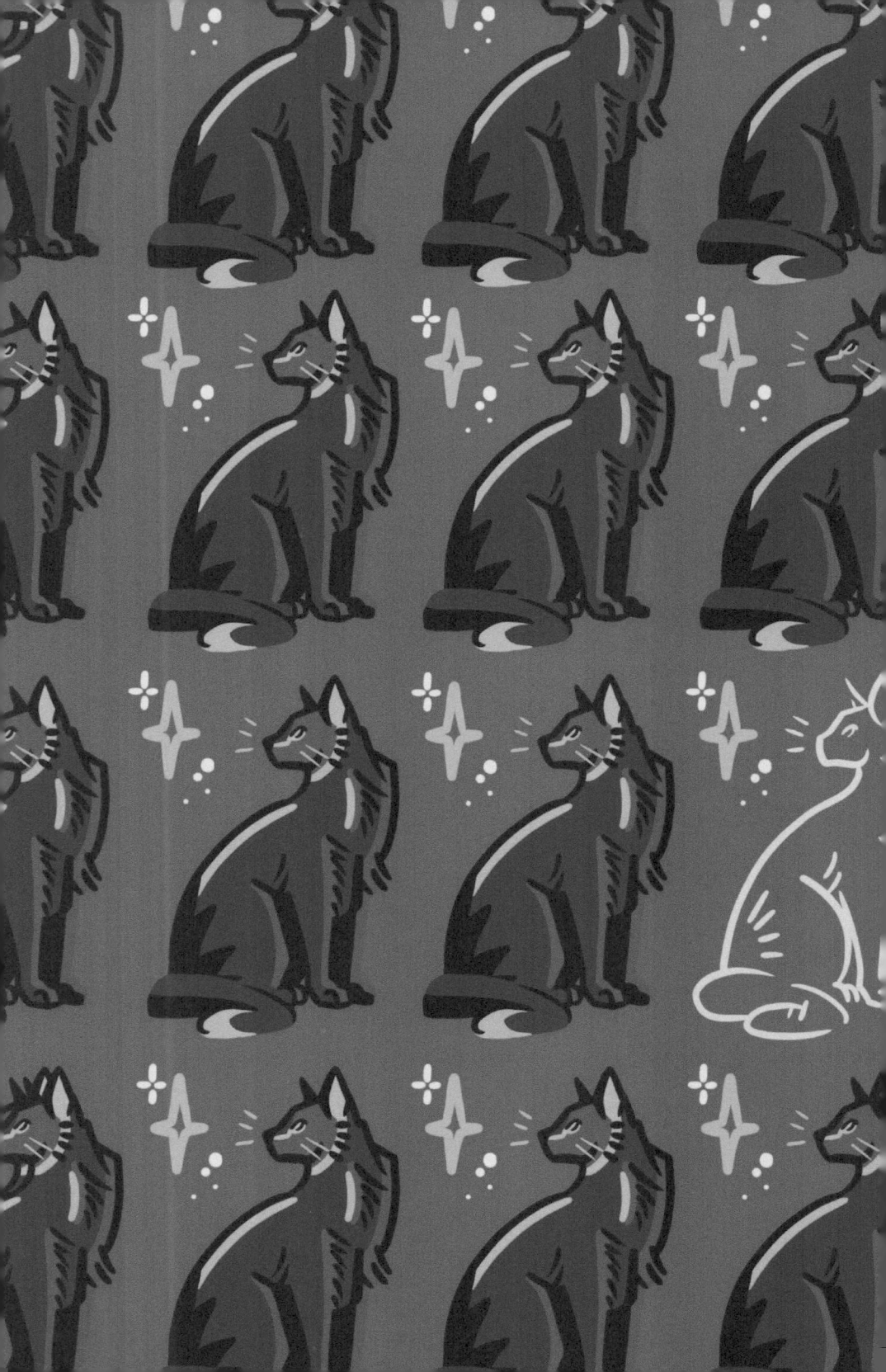

Rejection as a Stray Cat

She lurks.

Though she is quiet,
She is nestled in brick and sawdust,
And the clouds are charcoal,
And the sky is ready to sketch a storm,
And our backyard is nothing but open concrete.
She demands our undivided attention.

Though she does not belong to us,
We can't help but open our hearts to her.

Night Sky

What if the stars aren't a guiding light?
We always try to find hope in the darkness,
But the light only shows us what we refuse to see.

Moving forward
Is only repeating
The past.

I will always fall
For someone
Who does not love me.

The first girl I ever loved
Was not someone
Worth loving.

Maybe, it wasn't love.
Maybe, it was only
Her,
Standing there,
Blank eyes,
Knowing there was no way
She could feel
The same.

The curdling in my stomach
Could have just been
The milky way.

The rosiness of my cheeks
Could have just been
Heat stroke,

Except the sun was not shining
Because it was nighttime, and even the sun

Could not produce the kind of warmth she did.

Imagine her the night sky, and me, the stars;
I could only shine in her darkness, and
How could that not be love?

Maybe, it wasn't love.
Maybe, it was only
Her,
Standing there,
Blank eyes,
As I showed her
My cuts.

Maybe, it wasn't love.
Maybe, it was only
Her,
Standing there,
Blank eyes,
Not knowing how to treat me,
So she just didn't treat me
At all.

Imagine her the night sky, and me, the stars;
In a crowded city, only the streetlights
Guide us home.

Ode to Camila Cabello Ending in a Swarm of Bees

Right now I'm shameless,
Which is something I seldom am,
But *I've been running from it for the longest time* now,
Because shame is my heartbeat
Pounding against my ribcage;
I can only escape it in my dreams.

A *choir singing hallelujah* hides in the corner of the classroom,
Chanting the useless plea,
As you and I make eye contact.
There's God in every move your eyes make,
Averting mine.
I've never believed in God,
But if He's anything like you,
Then I'm glad I don't worship Him
Anymore.

Sometimes words are not enough to describe the way,
Honey dripping from your lips,
Your canines twinkle in the moonlight;
A black bear on the hunt
For human flesh.

You're the living proof
Some bodies are meant
To crumble, like feta:
Neither of us are Greek, but
Our bodies must be
If my heart can break
So easily at the sight
Of your sticky lips,
Your lifeless eyes.

I was not living, I was just writing about it until you came up to me on that dance floor,
Took me by the hand, only to say goodbye.

I was not living until you showed me
How expansive the feeling of loneliness can be.

I was not living until the honey that dripped from your lips
Seeped through my clothing,
Staining my skin.

I was not living until the bees stung me raw,
And I told them,
*"Maybe you should set me free,
Maybe I don't really want you to."*

Drunken Ramblings of a Broken Heart

If I were to spill my heart on this page, every word would merely be your name. Cut me open, and you would find the love letters I never had the courage to write, tangled in my intestines. Though they may be bloody, the letters are as crisp as the daydreams that blind my nights- streetlamps down the boulevard of organs. My dreams feed my cerebrum pictures of you smiling at me. I only think of you when I'm dreaming. In my dreams, I live through what high school could have been if I hadn't come out of the closet. Every night, we were still friends. This is no metaphor. Maybe, had it not been you who had taken this heart, you would not have had to dash from the crime scene. I wonder why my body always ends up being the crime scene; why I am only a burial ground of your most fatal flaws. Do you even remember them? When I hold them up to the light, it's hard to distinguish your flaws from your attributes. What am I saying? You are the streetlamp on a boulevard I have driven past long ago. I barely know you. You were my friend once, ten years ago.

Rejection as a Manic Episode

"I'm okay," she says,
"I've never felt better,"
But we are not entirely convinced.

We see the bags under her eyes,
Filled with the $200 worth of ice cream she bought,
Didn't have room in the freezer for, so
She just
Ate it all.

We don't know if it's been days,
Or weeks,
Since she's last showered.

She's gotten out of bed, sure,
But when will she return
Without a lover?

"I'm okay," she says,
"I've never felt better,"
But we don't know,
Is she trying to convince us,
Or herself?

Museum

I know
That some carcasses
Are never recovered,
But my fossils were put up
On display for everyone to examine.
Missing were the informative plaques,
Letting my peers come to their own conclusions.

One told me she would find me a therapist when I told her
I'm gay.

Another told me to stop joking about something so serious,
And wouldn't believe me for months.

I got anonymous messages telling me
To kill myself.

When someone else decided to bully me,
She specifically told me it wasn't because I'm gay,
Which makes me believe that it was.

Someone I once considered a friend
Decided to spread a rumour
That I had raped her,
Which was probably only believable
Because of my sexuality.

I don't know how to write these childhood traumas
In metaphor.

I don't know how to dull the blade
Of the knife they used to decapitate me.

I don't know how to say this
In a way that is easy to digest.

I hope you can sit
With the heartburn
This poem gives you,
And understand that, while I wished you were gay,
I wouldn't wish this
On anybody.

Instincts
====

After Sarah Kay

The body has this instinct to live even when the mind has the instinct to die & It was June 15th & a friend told me you might take it personally if I killed myself, so that night I texted you *that if I ever died it wouldn't be your fault*, because it wasn't & still I tried to strangle myself & I didn't know yet that it never would have worked because the neural pathways will direct the hands to stop, even though I didn't want to stop & you didn't know either & it was exam season & we both should have been studying, but how could we study in the face of all of this pain & fear & you never answered my text & you didn't look me in the eye the next day when I showed up for the exam & I mean, you hadn't looked me in the eye in months & that didn't make it hurt any less & I only know you told your parents what I'd sent you & they told the school because, after the exam, I got called to the guidance counsellor's office & she called my family & she sent us to the hospital & I texted you to thank you, even though I didn't really mean it, because the body has this instinct to live even when the mind has the instinct to die & I got sent home from the hospital that night because I told the psychiatrist I didn't want to kill myself anymore & I didn't mean it & I still don't & we never spoke of it again.

My Burgundy Dreams

She walked so gracefully, her hair, ringlets
Down her back. Her eyes captivated me
The way the mud captivates a piglet.
Call her a bath for my burgundy dreams.
She smiled, lips closed, keeping her mystery.
The secrets in her teeth could bring me to
My knees, but if I had the liberty,
I would pry them from her mouth; play a tune
To their melancholy, and release them
To the wild. I once kept my promises,
But she led me to wear what she condemned
As the flag of my people. Ominous,
I know. Let me explain how she destroyed;
Cascading through clouds, she glided with poise.

Cascading through clouds, she glided with poise,
But in her hands was my still beating heart.
I wonder if, when she met with the boys
She loved more than me, she'd show them my art.
Paint splattered across the room, nothing but
Canvas to keep me warm, I drew her name
Into the floor, the walls, even my cuts.
She couldn't know how, without her, I became
A scavenger for a breathing, living
Soul, who could hear my pain, sit with me, and
Tell me I am loved. I'm not forgiving
Of the sins committed, though were not planned.
She tells me she wishes to be sinless.
I can say, because of her, I'm wingless.

I can say, because of her, I'm wingless.
Because she plucked me feather by feather,
Created necklaces for the mindless,
And left me with nothing but the letters
I wrote to her every day, in every
Class. I know she couldn't help herself, and read
Every word of my broken reverie.
Many days, I wish I had not been fed
Her toenails; her dry skin; her soft earwax;
The parts she had already left behind.
Still, they tasted to my lips like peach schnapps;
Sweet, and young, unlike wine that is refined.
She did not listen, couldn't help but destroy
An angel fallen without any noise.

An angel fallen without any noise;
She graced this earth with a presence
Even an atheist like me enjoys,
But can never have. I thanked the heavens
I could never reach for bringing her close
To me, even though I could not relish
In her glory. I was a ghost, arose
From the ground to guide her. She was selfish
And didn't want to return home. Rather, she
Wished to remain on Earth, tempted by friends
Who made her feel careless, reckless, and free.
I wanted to follow her to the ends
Of the galaxy, I was so entranced.
She left me, without so much as a glance.

She left me, without so much as a glance,
I hoped due to peer pressure, but I know
In her mind, it was a delicate dance
Between being strong, and letting it show
That she really did care for me, at least
Enough to ensure I did not perish,
Wither in a coffin, become a feast
For the insects. Did she ever cherish
The moments we spent together the way
I did? Did she miss me? Does it even
Matter? Whether she left me to decay
Or not is irrelevant. Believe in
Me when I say she cut me loose, not free,
Because I liked her more than she liked me.

Because I liked her more than she liked me,
I was treated differently by all
Who knew. I had friends who turned out to be
Bullies, leaving me on my knees to crawl
Back to her, though she could not have cared less.
I was the fly in her hair, she wanted
To swat me away and to leave no mess,
But I stuck to the wall 'til I rotted.
Not that anybody noticed, or if
They did, they left me to burn in sunlight;
A vampire seeking redemption. The stiff
Board I was bound to was left out all night.
I asked her to come save me in advance.
She refused to even give me a chance.

She refused to even give me a chance
At being her friend, because I was weird,
And she was popular. How could she prance
About the hallway when I disappeared
From her life? She showed me she was happy,
Better off without me, so I believed
It. I left until her voice got raspy
Calling for me, and when I let her breathe,
I thanked her, but she was already gone.
She built herself a fortress away from
The drama, and pain. When we reached the dawn
She did not peak out her window, didn't come
Out to play in the green field with the trees.
She locked up her heart and threw out the key.

She locked up her heart and threw out the key.
I learned to pick locks, but she hid the hole
In her nightmares; even her darkest dreams
Did not manifest me. I searched the whole
Town, but could not find her sleeping. Instead,
I found her guards watching for me, haunting
The streets, looking down on me as I bled
Roses. Even that didn't stop the taunting.
Nothing could stop the taunting from the kids
Who ripped me out the closet, still naked,
Pried open my chest, plucked each of my ribs,
Just to fill the hole she left with hatred.
When she did not let my heart off the hook,
I scrambled to find it in every nook.

I scrambled to find it in every nook,
But I lost the will to live without her.
I tried, and tried, until the ceiling shook,
But still, I could not find what we once were
Within the depths of my lungs. Rather, the
Asphyxiation sent me spiralling
Down, and down, below rock bottom, where a
Crush like mine on her was not worth having,
Where the shit festered so deeply in my
Skin, I turned into one; a living turd
Whose purpose was to be flushed and to die
In the sewers. My ideas were blurred
Because I searched for a hope in this mess,
Though it was nowhere to be seen, I guess.

Though it was nowhere to be seen, I guess
I didn't need it anyway. Besides, who
Needs hope when I have someone who can bless
My desk space with the scent of her perfume?
Who needs hope when hope is not nearly as
Beautiful as her eyes; twinkling stars that
Shoot past me faster than the blue topaz
Of the ocean? If only we could chat
Now. If only she understood my pain.
I didn't need her to save me, but to hug
Me, break the chain connecting to my brain,
Grinding against my will to live. She dug
Up a trench instead. That was when I looked.
I found something better in this notebook.

I found something better in this notebook:
A world in which she could learn to love me,
But her closest allies were crooks, and took
My privacy away. I must agree,
I wasn't worth the luxury. I wasn't worth
The silver nails hammered in the coffin
Containing my dreams. I crumbled in earth,
Fed myself to the worms, let them soften
My desires into mulch, became fodder
For all those to come who were not liked back.
Let it be known that this is a slaughter
Of every lost soul, every bone that cracks
For someone else's undeserved happiness.
Call it what you want, I'll call it progress.

Call it what you want, I'll call it progress
That now, she follows me on Instagram.
I must confess, it does not stop the stress
I used to have when I'd see her. Goddamn
My heart, how it beats for her still, after
All this time and suffering. I doubt she
Even realizes how her shy laughter
Makes the world stutter, at least for a beat.
I feel it as my head hits the pillow
After a hard day. I don't care what they
Say. I'll let her be the silent killer
If I can see her smile. I'm really gay,
So call me a sinner, call me the sun,
The way I can see myself for someone.

The way I can see myself for someone
Is astonishing, considering how
She never seemed to. Maybe, I am done
Letting her steal the show, so take a bow
For the appearance in my life story.
I'm no sidekick, but a motherfucking
Protagonist. I'll take all the glory
For surviving this life and suffering.
All I'll leave her with is the knowledge that
She will always be my muse, my divine
Inspiration. I'm ready to combat
Anybody who will not let me shine,
At least, that is until I find someone
Who is worth more than the harm she has done.

Who is worth more than the harm she has done
If not me? She would likely refuse it,
But maybe, it's also her. Anyone
Can see that, perhaps, if I had not slit
My wrists for her, she would still talk to me.
Maybe it was not that I liked her, but
That I came on too strong for her to see
I was just a squirrel, looking for a nut:
Any girl would do. I needed her as
A friend far more than as a meal. I could
Starve if it meant I could be what she has.
As I told her this in my dreams, she stood.
Though the possibilities were limitless,
She walked so gracefully, her hair, ringlets.

She walked so gracefully, her hair, ringlets;
Cascading through clouds, she glided with poise.
I can say, because of her, I'm wingless;
An angel fallen without any noise.
She left me, without so much as a glance,
Because I liked her more than she liked me.
She refused to even give me a chance.
She locked up her heart and threw out the key.
I scrambled to find it in every nook,
Though it was nowhere to be seen. I guess,
I found something better in this notebook.
Call it what you want, I'll call it progress,
The way I can see myself for someone
Who is worth more than the harm she has done.

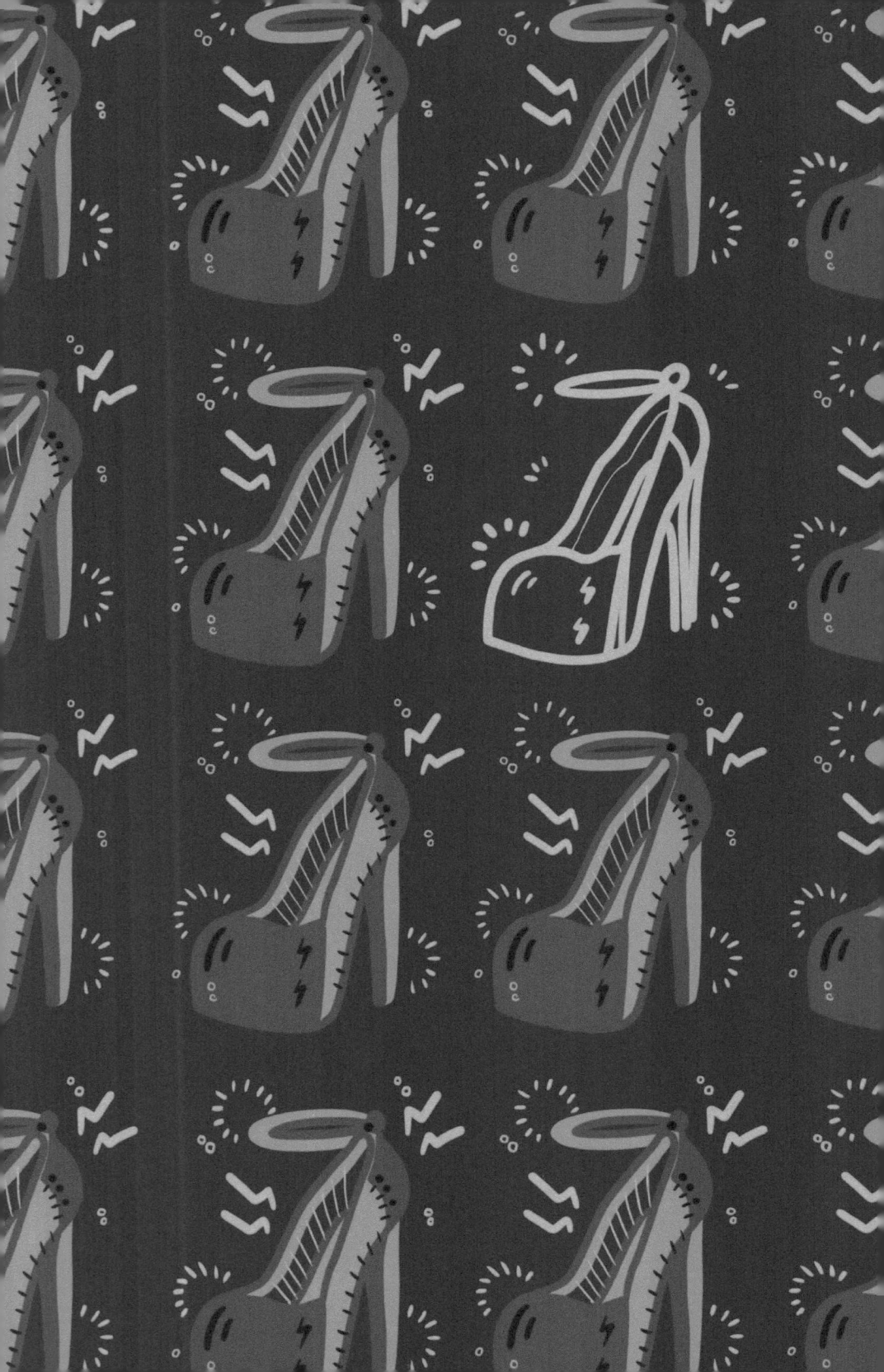

Rejection as a Drag Queen

She definitely puts on a show.

The flashing lights-
The garments-
The death drops
That make us feel
Our hearts stop-
How could we not be
Awestruck?

We have to remember,
Though she gets the notes right
Every time,
She is not the one singing.

We Were All Just Stars on Fire

A condom full of semen
Isn't the most romantic token,
But here I am, anyway,
In a nice hotel room
In a shady part of town,
Cleaning up after the boy
Who just came
And left.

I think the testosterone has led me to also be attracted to men.
I wonder what my twelve-year-old self
Would say to me now.

Yes, I know,
I am not any less queer for this,
But after all the hard work I went through
To accept myself for liking you,
It feels like I've thrown it all away.

I dig through the trash.
I find the novels I wrote
About a world in which you and I ended up together.
I wonder what would have happened
Had we actually dated.

I imagine they would have eaten you alive.

I didn't come out of the closet on purpose.
I stumbled out the doors,
Scarves in my mouth,
Belts in my hands,
After someone else flung them open.
By the time I shed what wasn't mine,
Everyone was gawking.

Their whispers were cicadas singing
To the setting sun.
When I was a child, I believed
The sound was of the sun itself, warning us
That one day, we too
Would be a star on fire.

There was no elephant in this room,
Merely insects crawling
Into people's ears.
I decided to be honest.
They could not hear me over the buzz.

I was not accepted for being queer.
I was tolerated.

I was not the closet.
I was the dining room.

I was not a person.
I was the representation of an entire community stuffed
Within a body,
Splayed out on the table,
Apple between my teeth.

How could I not feel
The weight of everyone's expectations
Without becoming what I thought they wanted?

You and I both know
I was not the only queer person at that school,
Even if I was the only one out.
We were all just stars on fire;
No one could hear our truths
When they were too busy playing
With cicadas.
Just because I was visible,

Does not mean that they saw me
For me.

I'm not saying I still wish we dated.
I'm saying
Thank whatever higher power is out there
That we didn't.

If I Were an Artist

I would find you
A rough sketch
Of the person you were meant to become.

When I would go to cut you off the page,
You would take the razor from my hand
And slit your own wrist.

This is what I am most afraid of-
That, in exposing you to my pain,
I showed you how to cope with your own.

13 Ways of Looking at a Memory
After Wallace Stevens

I -
I didn't even notice the thumping
Of bass when your fingers grazed my forearm,
I mistook it for my heartbeat
and I could have sworn
That when you looked into my eyes,
Every kid in that gymnasium,
Searching for a feeling even half as intoxicating,
Vanished.

II -
When the black car pulled in to pick me up from my first school dance,
I was old enough to know I liked you, but I was a girl,
And you are a girl.

III -
I've never been one with sticky fingers
But daily, I would risk it all for a stolen glance.

IV -
For a month, during lunch, I sat by the trees,
Watching their leaves kiss the soccer field,
Thinking about phases;
How this was definitely not one of them.
I spent the next month slowly coming out to friends.
Friends who told you;
You who quickly cut me out of your life,
You who spent all your time proving how much you liked boys.

V -
The silence between us was so loud,
I'd cover my ears each time you walked by,

But that didn't stop me from overhearing you
Telling the new girl I was weird.

VI -
You once told me you were a bee without a stinger,
But you turned out to be a wasp.

VII -
But it was me who etched your name into my forearm,
Wore your initials as jewelry, my love- an open secret.

VIII -
I texted you
> *If I ever die, it won't be your fault.*

You did not respond.

The next morning,
When the guidance counselor called me into her office,
I sighed with relief;
At least I knew you'd read it.

IX -
At the hospital, I lied to the psychiatrist and she sent me home.

X -
I no longer recall if we spoke after that.

By graduation you were just another white gown in the crowd.

XI -
I've silenced your name with tattoos.

XII -

I dip my fingers in honey each day and paint my skin with sweetness.

XIII -
I dye my hair in a bathroom, here,
In a city six hours away from where we met
When a song comes on the radio, a familiar thumping,
And I realize I haven't thought about you in ten years.

Acknowledgements

Thank you to the staff of the publications in which the following poems have appeared:

> *mcsway's Heartbreak Museum 3rd Edition:* "Drunken Ramblings of a Broken Heart"
>
> *Anti-Heroin Chic:* "Instincts"

Thank you to Sierra De Mulder and Neil Hilborn for hosting the workshops that generated the majority of this collection.

Thank you to Catherine Black, Sabrina Benaim, Aimee Caron, Mickey Vranic, Christina Brown, Samantha Lapenna, and anyone else who took the time to help me make my thoughts cohesive.

Thank you to Pam for not only inspiring me to bring an artist onboard, but for being that artist who brought this project to the next level. Her work has always inspired me, and to collaborate with her has been a dream come true.

Thank you to anyone who believed I could do this. I would never have been confident enough to release this collection without them.

About the Author & Artist

The Author

    Cameron Chiovitti has always been different. They felt it most when they came out as a lesbian at twelve-years-old, in an all-girls private Catholic high school in Montreal, QC. It's safe to say Cameron was the only 2SLGBTQ+ person they knew for a long time. As the years have gone by, they've met people who make them feel like they belong. They felt safe enough to come out as nonbinary at nineteen. Cameron currently attends OCAD University in Toronto, ON for creative writing. While they don't ascribe themselves to any one particular community, they believe they've found pieces of community everywhere they've been. They can be found online @maskofpoetry.

The Artist

    Pamela Leszczynski is an emerging multi-disciplinary artist currently based in Toronto, ON. Most notably known for her creative platform @wildfirepunch, she works in tattooing, painting, photography, illustration, sculpture and multi-media installation exploring the shifting landscape present in the self and nature through bold and colourful aesthetics. As a self-identified gender fluid member of the queer community, her own personal experience of being queer is a continual process, and she is continuously striving to work alongside other queer creatives to bring more exposure and understanding for the 2SLGBTQ+ community.

CPSIA information can be obtained
at www.ICGtesting.com
Printed in the USA
LVHW070436060721
691874LV00001B/248